Presented to:

____

____

____

Never Forget The Difference You've Made

Made in the USA
Monee, IL
13 December 2019

18546360R00066